The Bubble Brigade

www.emkidsbooks.com

page
vision

228 Hamilton Ave.,
Palo Alto, CA 94301

The Bubble Brigade

Teaching Children the Concept of Personal Space
and how to Protect Themselves

EDWARD L. MARTIN JR. M.S

This book is dedicated to the Wallenpaupack
Area High School class of 2005.

They were the first Buckhorn Bubble Brigadiers
and were followed by many more!

Mountain Lake Elementary School was a great place for its students and staff. The students loved their teachers, and their teachers felt the same way about the students. The food in the cafeteria was good, and the playground was terrific. However, the school had one problem—a big one...and it was growing.

There were way too many students with bumps and bruises being sent to the school nurse and principal. Some were accidental; some were not. The students were being to "handsy"–doing too much pushing, shoving, and even kicking and hitting each other. This was not only happening at recess but also in the hallways, cafeteria, and even in the classrooms. Clearly, something had to be done. That happened when Mr. Carter, the school counselor, started visiting the classrooms.

"Good morning, boys and girls. How are things in kindergarten?" asked Mr. Carter with his customary smile.

"Good morning, Mr. Carter," replied Mrs. DeLong's class. The students enjoyed their counselor's visits because they never knew what he was going to teach them, and his lessons were usually fun.

"What are we going to learn about today?" inquired the inquisitive Tyler.

"Well, T-man," joked Mr. Carter, "let's see if you and your classmates can figure out what our lesson is about today." With that, he drew a circle on the board with what looked like a person inside the circle.

"Is that a person?" asked Claire.

"That is right, Claire. What is the person inside?" asked Mr. Carter.

"A circle," called out several students.

"Kind of," said their counselor. Then he pretended to blow air through something, and Brian said, "It's a bubble!"

"Bingo," laughed Mr. Carter. "Did you know all living things have a bubble around them? It's invisible so you can't see it, and it gets bigger and smaller depending on what is on the outside of it."

The class looked confused and dubious, so Mr. Carter continued to explain.

"Have you ever tried to sneak up on a bunny rabbit in your backyard? How about get close to a chipmunk or a butterfly or even a frog in a pond or stream? What do they all do when you get too close?" asked the counselor.

"They take off," said Ruby. "They fly, run, or swim away, right, Mr. Carter?"

"You are correct, Ruby Dubey Do! And the reason is that the bubble that protects them is warning them that they may be in danger," explained Mr. Carter. "Does that make sense?" he asked further.

Most of the students nodded, and he said, "Now we are going to find out some things about our own bubbles."

Mr. Carter asked Mrs. DeLong to stand on one side of the classroom. He started on the other side of the room and gradually approached her, stopping occasionally to ask how she was feeling. She replied that she felt fine, and Mr. Carter said, "Mrs. DeLong, when you start to feel uncomfortable, tell me to stop." When he got about an arm's length away, she asked him to stop.

"You see, class. I just bumped up against your teacher's bubble. She felt uncomfortable because I was a bit too close. I was in her personal space," he said. "Now I want you to watch your teacher's bubble get much bigger." He turned out the classroom lights and went back across the room away from their teacher. "Let's imagine its nighttime, and Mrs. DeLong is walking through the park all alone. Let's also imagine I am a stranger approaching her, not someone she knows. Does everyone understand? Let's see what happens to her bubble now."

Mr. Carter did not even get halfway across the room before Mrs. DeLong asked him to stop.

"Look at how big your teacher's bubble is now," said their counselor. "Kiddos, does your teacher ever give you a pat on the back when you have made a good

choice or maybe a high-five? Or how about a hug when you are upset? When she does that, is it okay with you? Would you let someone you don't know do that? Probably not, because you don't trust them like you trust your teacher," he said.

"Now, can we imagine you are all looking out your classroom window because you heard some loud noises? As you are watching, you see trees falling over and you hear a loud roar getting closer and closer to school. Then suddenly, you see what is knocking trees over and roaring. It's a Tyrannosaurus rex! And it's looking right at your class as it moves toward you. Do you think your bubble would get bigger real fast? Would it be telling you to get away real fast?"

The whole class called out, "Yes!"

"So you all understand how your invisible bubble protects you, right?" asked the counselor. When the students replied "yes," he asked them who was in charge of their bubbles.

Karsyn raised her hand. "We are, each one of us, right, Mr. Carter?" she answered quickly.

"Absolutely, Karsyn," he replied. "Each of you can decide for yourself if you are going to let Grandma give you a smoochie," he laughingly told them. The class all laughed with him.

"It is important we respect each other's personal space. We need to keep our hands and feet to ourselves and not be pulling, pushing, hitting, or kicking anybody else. High-fives, pats on the back, playing tag, and such are usually all right if everyone is okay with them," he told them.

"What if we're playing tag at recess and tag someone or even knock them down. Is that breaking someone's bubble in a bad way?" asked Tyson.

I'm sorry.

"Good question, Tyson, I am glad you asked it," answered Mr. Carter. "An accident means something happened you didn't mean to happen—you didn't plan it or do it deliberately. If something like that happens, you help the person back up and say you are sorry. That way, the person will know you didn't mean it. I will be back next week to teach you how to protect yourself. Meanwhile, I expect to hear we are having less problems with bubble-breaking, okay?" he asked.

The students all nodded yes, and off he went to his next class.

When he came to class the following week, the students were very excited. They remembered he had told them he was going to teach them how to protect themselves. What kind of self-defense was he going to show them...kung fu, judo, karate?

"Class," he said to them, "step number 1 in knowing how to protect yourself is learning how to use Brave Talk."

"What is Brave Talk, Mr. Carter?" asked Lily.

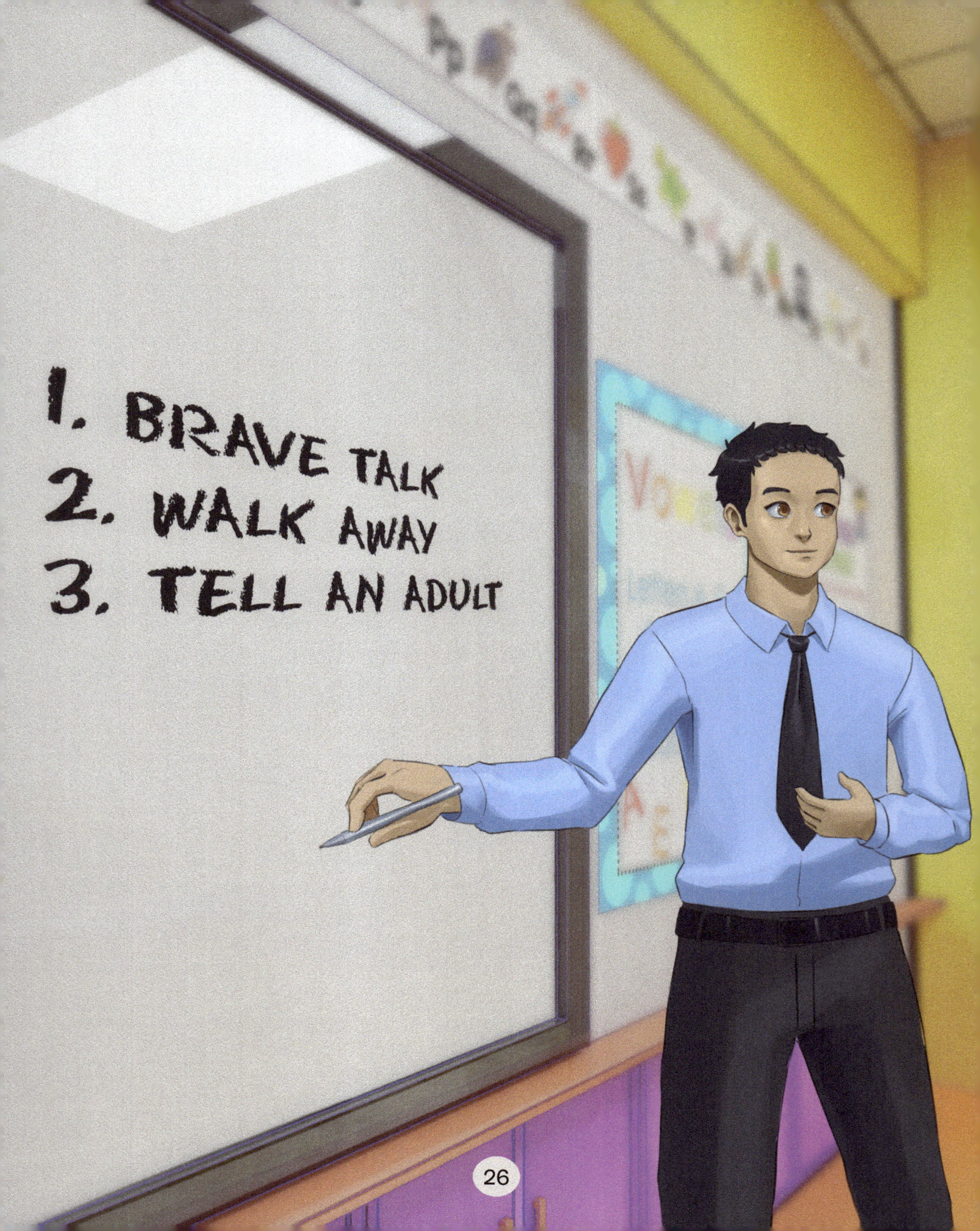
1. BRAVE TALK
2. WALK AWAY
3. TELL AN ADULT

"Well, if someone is doing something to you that you don't like, that is when you use your Brave Talk. Some examples are when someone is calling you names, pushing you, taking your crayons without asking, that kind of thing. Here is how it works. You look the person right in the eye, don't smile, and tell them exactly what it is that you want them to stop. If someone is calling you names, you say, 'I don't like it when you call me names. Please stop.'"

"But, Mr. Carter, what do you do if the person doesn't stop?" asked Shameer.

"Then, Shameer, you walk away from them, and if they follow you and keep doing it, you tell an adult. You also should tell the adult you asked them to stop and walked away, and they kept doing it. You know who would be in trouble then, right? So our three steps in protecting ourselves are no. 1, use Brave Talk; no. 2, walk away; and no. 3, tell an adult. Does that make sense?" asked Mr. Carter.

"We got it, Mr. Carter," answered Natalie for the class.

"Now that you all understand about our bubbles and how to protect yourself, I guess you can be allowed to join the Mountain Lake Bubble Brigade," announced their counselor. "Everyone, stand up, raise your right hand, and say, 'I promise not to break anyone's bubble in a mean way.'"

The class did as he asked, although they did look a bit confused. When they were done, Mr. Carter said, "Mrs. DeLong, will you please show the class our chart now?"

Mrs. DeLong brought out a large sheet of poster board. It had enough circles drawn on it for each member of the class. Each circle (or bubble) had one of the student's names on it. These circles were also divided up into four pieces.

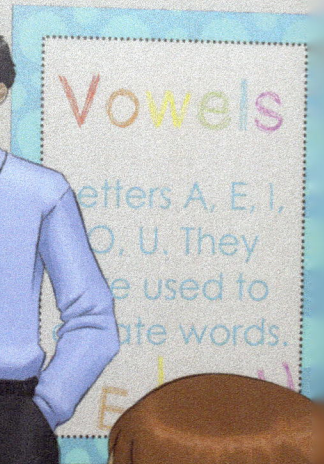

"These are your Bubble Brigade badges class. If you break someone's bubble in a mean way, Mrs. DeLong will draw a checkmark in the first spot on your badge. We have four marking periods in the school year, which is why your badge is divided up into four parts. I will be coming into class all year, and I will be checking your badges. At the end of every marking period, I will bring a surprise for the students who don't have more than two marks on their badge. As the school year goes on, in each marking period, I will bring in a different surprise, but you will have to have less marks on your badge to get a surprise. Does everyone understand?" asked Mr. Carter.

The class was excited when Mr. Carter left. As the rest of the school year progressed, a funny thing started happening. There was less and less "bubble-popping" and much more "niceness" spreading through the school. Mountain Lake Elementary had become a great place to go to school to!

www.ingramcontent.com/pod-product-compliance
Lightning Source LLC
Chambersburg PA
CBHW042334030426
42335CB00027B/3343